Embracing

The

Journey

of

Recovery

FROM

TRAGEDY

TO

TRIUMPH

DR. LARRY SMITH

NEW YORK

EMBRACING THE JOURNEY OF RECOVERY

© 2007 Dr. Larry Smith

ISBN: 978-1-60037-241-4 (Paperback)
ISBN: 978-1-60037-242-1 (Hardcover)

Published by:

Creative Genius
An Imprint of Morgan James Publishing, LLC
1225 Franklin Ave Ste 325
Garden City, NY 11530-1693
Toll Free 800-485-4943
www.MorganJamesPublishing.com

Cover and Interior Design by:
Tony Laidig
www.thecoverexpert.com
tony@thecoverexpert.com

About the Author

Dr. Larry Smith has practiced chiropractic for 19 years on beautiful Vancouver Island, Canada. His mission is to promote the tremendous benefits of chiropractic, health and fitness for the whole family. He uses his diversified life experiences to help his patients reach their maximum healing potential and strongly encourages every person to take responsibility for his or her own health. On Sunday August 27, 2006, he competed in the Subaru Ironman Canada Triathlon to help raise money for those suffering from chemical dependency.

Dr. Larry is a published author and was featured in Aspatore Publication's recently released *Inside the Minds: The Art and Science of Sports Medicine.*

His *Fitness Prescription DVD* is being utilized by his colleagues all across Canada and is also being viewed in over 30 different countries.

You can contact Dr. Larry by email at: drlarr@shaw.ca

Dedication

This book is dedicated to my Mom (Pauline) and Laurie's Mom (Anny). May we one day possess the courage you have both shown us on your respective journeys.

Table of Contents

Prologue

It is a daunting task to compile and assimilate the vast amount of literature on the subject of recovery from a life threatening illness or injury. The challenge lays in taking a very multifaceted and immense subject and somehow reducing it to only its most crucial elements. That's when I remembered a speech I heard from Zig Ziglar many years ago. The following excerpt is taken from Zig Ziglar's book "See You at the Top."

We must teach our children the wisdom of the ages. What is that? Zig Ziglar tells the story of how the wisdom of the ages was discovered.

Many years ago, a wise old king called his wise men together and gave them a commission. "I want you to compile for me the wisdom of the ages. Put it in book form so we might leave it to posterity."

The wise men left the king and worked for a long period of time. They finally returned with twelve volumes and proudly proclaimed that this truly was "the wisdom of the ages." The king looked at the twelve volumes and said, "Gentlemen, I'm certain this is the wisdom of the ages and that it contains the knowledge we should leave to mankind. However, it is too long and I fear that people will not read it. Condense it!"

Embracing the Journey of Recovery

Again the wise men worked long and hard before they returned with only one volume. The king, however, knew that it was still too lengthy so he commanded them to further condense their work. The wise men reduced the volume to a chapter, then to a page, then to a paragraph, and finally to a sentence. When the wise old king saw the sentence he was absolutely elated. "Gentlemen," he said, "this is truly the wisdom of the ages, and as soon as all men everywhere learn this truth, then most of our problems will be solved."

The sentence simply said, "There Ain't No Free Lunch."

As a health care practitioner, I have experienced the joys of seeing my patients regain their lost health and return to a life of meaning. Along the way, I have also experienced the heartbreak and anguish of patients who were unable to recover from a life threatening injury or illness.

I am both humbled and honored to bring you my experience, strength and hope of *Embracing the Journey of Recovery*. It is my intention that the readers will not have to wade through unnecessary detail; I'll get right to the point. However, it is imperative for any person recovering from a life threatening injury or illness to work on their recovery program each and every day. Remember, **"There Ain't No Free Lunch."**

Introduction

I want to inspire you to embrace the journey of recovery. The road to recovery can be a long and arduous process that involves heart-break, obstacles, challenges and unexpected complications. However the rewards of a triumphant recovery are astonishing and will absolutely transform your life. In the beginning of the process, it is natural to feel overwhelmed, discouraged, disheartened and defeated. That is why it is absolutely essential to keep your focus on a positive outcome. If you have faith confidence and belief in a power greater than yourself and absolute certainty about your purpose in life, you can and will recover from your life threatening illness.

By reading this book and "Embracing the Journey of Recovery" you will:

- Drastically improve your relationships

- Learn how to save your soul by baring your soul

- Positively impact the lives of others while you are still wounded

- Experience the absolute magic of a close knit support group

- Harness the incredible power of your personal heroes

- Count your blessings in turbulent times

Embracing the Journey of Recovery

- Realize why pain is necessary for you to fully recover

- See first hand how visualization can build bridges, moves mountains and drastically improve your speed of recovery

- Learn the principle of Kaizen and have more energy, vitality and zest for life than ever before

- Be prepared to face the ultimate challenge of your recovery program

- Have the courage to face your demons and conquer them

THE CHALLENGE OF GETTING STARTED

What are some of the challenges facing you when you are recovering from a serious injury or life threatening illness?

Here are some common questions and comments heard from individuals beginning to embark on their journey of recovery.

"What am I going to do?"

"How do I get started?"

"Who do I ask for help?"

"I just don't see how I will ever get better."

"How can I exercise when it hurts so much that I can barely move?"

"I'm very despondent; I don't think there is any hope for me and my family."

"Why bother trying?"

"I'd be better off dead!"

"I'm humiliated. Some people enjoy kicking me when I'm down."

"Who can I trust when I feel so vulnerable?"

"If only the pain would go away for just a little while!"

"What did I do to deserve this?"

The major challenge for most recovering individuals is coping with physical pain. If you have physical pain and it hurts like hell, it is very likely that you are unable to work. If you are unable to work, it is quite possible that you also have financial difficulties.

In fact it is not uncommon to hear the following complaints all at once.

"I am in constant, excruciating pain. I am unable to work and I may never work again. I am so afraid of what is going to happen to me. I have no energy and I am so grouchy that my partner can't stand being around me for more than five minutes. I'm miserable and I am going broke! What am I going to do? Will somebody please help me? God, where are you?"

WHAT ARE THE BASIC NEEDS OF THE RECOVERING INDIVIDUAL?

At the very least, the basic needs of the recovering individual include:

- Pain relief
- A reason to recover

- Direction

- A coach or mentor

- Motivation

- Support

- Signs of improvement

- Confidence

- A plan

- HOPE (The #1 key ingredient to recovery)

THE MESSAGE OF HOPE

"Embrace the Journey of Recovery" is a journey of focus. The focus is not about what has happened to you nor is it a contest of who has the most pain, worst trauma or serious disease.

To each person suffering from a life threatening injury or illness, his or her situation seems the worst!

The focus is on the present and what an individual can do to move forward. This book not only explores the issues of the recovering individual but actually confronts the many problems and dilemmas that will inevitably arise. The key element is to embark upon the journey with a balanced approach of the mind, body and spirit. The whole person is injured in mind, body and spirit. Therefore, the recovery of the whole person also involves the mind, body and spirit. One cannot function independently of the other. The mind, body and spirit are interconnected at all times.

Hope for the best, plan for the worst and expect the unexpected. This book tells you how to get started, who to ask for help and where to ask for help. If you or a loved one is going through difficult and agonizing times, remember just one thing. There is always hope. You need only to look for it. It is never far away even if you think it is.

"Embrace the Journey of Recovery" will be experienced through two ordinary individuals who were faced with life threatening challenges. These characters are real individuals but their names, places and events have been altered to protect their identities. At many points during their recovery, they both wanted to give up and prayed daily about dying.

DONNY'S STORY

Donny was a 41 - year - old health professional with a promising future and a well established practice. He was a sports enthusiast and appeared happy and healthy — on the outside. However, after a bitter divorce, he finally realized that he had a serious problem with alcohol and other mood altering chemicals. He had contracted pneumonia, lost nearly 35 pounds and could barely walk before he gave up and finally asked for help. He was on a rapid downward spiral and just before he crashed, he wrote these thoughts and feelings in his journal.

"It was dismal, dark and damp outside which perfectly mirrored my inner world. Lying on the cold bathroom floor, I perceived that struggling, helpless boy from outside my body and wondered how he could escape. I have been hiding so many deep dark feelings for so long; and I now realize that I have just been masking my pain with alcohol. I need to get help and to find the courage to tell somebody my story. But I am so afraid and so

lonely. It seems that the grown man I have become can find no way to escape the feeling of pain, humiliation, hopelessness and despair. Who will listen to me? Who will believe my story? I feel much like the character described by T.S. Eliot in <u>The Love Song of J. Alfred Prufrock</u>. "I should've been a pair of ragged claws scuttling across the floors of silent seas."

Donny was a man who was fortunate enough to finally reach out and get help. You will experience his recovery from a life threatening condition in the upcoming chapters.

JOAN'S STORY

Joan was 53 years old and happily married to her second husband when she received the news that she had breast cancer. She was a very hard working, spirited, self sufficient registered nurse and a leader in her community. Since the cancer was progressing at an alarming rate, Joan had to undergo extensive chemotherapy and radiation before undergoing a bilateral mastectomy.

Following surgery, Joan lay awake one morning in a very fragile state and began to cry weakly. She looked into the mirror and saw an old, frail hag with no hair. She stared in disbelief at the bandages covering the incisions where her breasts used to be. Feelings of hopelessness and despair were overwhelming. She felt pain in every fiber of her being.

My career is gone. I am in agony. I don't even feel like a woman anymore. My situation is absolutely hopeless. I wish I were dead. Why has this happened to me? For the first time in my life, I honestly feel that there is no hope for me.

These were Joan's thoughts before she embarked on her incredible journey of recovery. To see a remarkably independent and strong woman reduced to a weak, cowering and sickly individual is very sobering. To follow the incredible journey of Joan's recovery is like witnessing a rebirth.

Joan and Donny have remarkable stories of recovery. They are ordinary individuals with tremendous humility and constant gratitude. Their message to you, the reader of this book, is that no matter how much pain and heartbreak you are experiencing, there is hope!

If you can relate to these two individuals in any way, you are in store for an incredible adventure.

Get ready, the journey is about to begin.

Why Asking for Help Is Absolutely Crucial

Why Asking for Help Is Absolutely Crucial

Finding a Higher Power (A Power Greater Than Yourself)

WHY IS IT SO IMPORTANT?

The challenging journey of recovery is extremely individual and entirely personal. No two journeys are exactly the same. Anyone who travels knows that a road map improves your chances of reaching your destination. It's the same with recovery. If you are recovering from a life threatening disease or severe injury and disability, there will be many rocky roads, bumps and obstacles to overcome. The first step is to find a power greater than yourself and have faith in that power.

As a veteran of over 14 marathons and 25 triathlons, Donny had extreme willpower and determination. Yet willpower only goes so far. Faith in a power greater than yourself is crucial and an absolute necessity to a successful recovery program.

Donny learned at a very young age that a person with faith in a higher power is a great deal stronger than a person without faith. One of his childhood heroes is still an icon in the sport of boxing. He is one of the greatest boxers of all time — Muhammad Ali. Nobody could ever accuse Muhammad of lacking self confidence. He is probably one of the brashest and most outspoken athletes of all time. Everyone remembers the quirky limericks that Ali used to taunt his opponents.

In an upcoming fight Muhammad Ali exclaimed "I'll be floating like a butterfly and stinging like a bee. I'll beat him so bad he'll need a shoehorn to put his hat on."

Even with his extreme "cocky" attitude, Muhammad Ali would always give thanks to his mighty God, "Allah" after each fight. (Muslims believe in One Almighty God, known by the proper name, Allah.) The key word in the last sentence is that he gave thanks to "his God." As long as you have faith in a power greater than yourself, you can call it whatever you want; God, Higher Power, Lord, Divine Power of the Universe or even Fred. The name of your higher power is totally up to you.

YOU DON'T HAVE TO DO IT ALONE

A major obstacle in Donny's early recovery was his apprehension towards the spiritual component of the AA program. He had faith in a higher power, but had a huge problem with organized religion. The priest from his former church was finally being brought to justice nearly 30 years later for sexually assaulting him and several other young boys. It was predictable and understandable that Donny's resentment ran very deep. During his stay at the treatment facility, Donny was instructed to simply find a <u>higher</u> power and believe in it. He did not have to believe in any religion or any other person's conception of God. He simply found a higher power and believed that it would help restore him to mental health and fitness.

THE STORY OF BILL W. AND ALCOHOLICS ANONYMOUS

In the Big Book of Alcoholics Anonymous, Bill W. and Dr. Bob describe the simplicity and the absolute crucial principle of having a faith in a power greater than ourselves.

"Much to our relief we discovered we did not need to consider another's conception of God. Our own conception, however inadequate, was sufficient to make the approach and to affect a contact with Him. As soon as we admitted the possible existence of a Creative Intelligence, a Spirit of the Universe underlying the totality of things, we began to be possessed of a new sense of power and direction, provided we took other simple steps. We found that God does not make too hard terms with those who seek him. To us, the Realm of Spirit is broad, roomy, all inclusive; never exclusive or forbidding to those who earnestly seek. It is open, we believe, to all...
...Do I now believe, or am I even willing to believe, that there is a Power greater than myself? As soon as a [person] can say that [they] do believe, or are willing to believe, we emphatically assure [them] that [they] are on [their] way. It has been repeatedly proven that from this simple cornerstone a wonderfully spiritual structure can be built. (Alcoholics Anonymous 4th Edition, p.46, 47)

Embracing the Journey of Recovery

The first key in recovery is to find a "higher power." It does not matter who or what it is called; just have one. I fully believe that a person who has faith in a divine being or higher power has a distinct advantage in their recovery process. It can come from the traditional religions and its teachings — but it is not a necessity.

TAPPING INTO YOUR HIGHER POWER
(THE POWER OF PRAYER)

How do you use your higher power once you have defined and believe in it? The answer is actually quite simple. Practice every day as if your life depends upon it. Simply ask for help and guidance as often as possible each day. Be grateful by giving thanks at each meal. Have faith in spite of your struggles and know that things are going to get better. Prayer is advocated and taught in nearly every religion and spiritual practice in the world. A simple yet powerful prayer practiced by AA groups throughout the world is the "The Serenity Prayer."

God grant me the Serenity
To accept the things I cannot change
Courage to change the things I can
And Wisdom to know the difference.

Dr. Larry Dossey is one of the foremost advocates of and experts in the power of prayer and its positive effects on health and healing. He states that there is plenty of scientific evidence, that prayer and faith are profound positive forces in recovery from life threatening illness and disability.

Dr. Dossey also expresses concern that North American society needs to move away from the notion that the only type of God that exists is a male, white, Anglo-Saxon Protestant, who speaks English. In fact many new AA members who are decidedly atheist or agnostic choose to use the AA group as their higher power. They call it G.O.D. This stands for <u>G</u>ood <u>O</u>rderly <u>D</u>irection.

Arguing about whether or not God exists is like fleas arguing about whether the dog exists; arguing about God's correct name is like fleas arguing about the name of the dog; and arguing over whose notion of God is correct is like fleas arguing about who owns the dog.

Robert Fulghum

THE POWER OF FORGIVENESS

Why bother praying or believing in a higher power? What about forgiving somebody who has hurt you? If you have ever questioned the power of prayer, the power of forgiving others or the power of God, I ask you to consider the incredible story of Immaculee Ilibagiza.

Immaculee Ilibagiza grew up in a country she loved, surrounded by a family she cherished. But in 1994 her world was ripped apart as Rwanda descended into bloody genocide. Immaculee's family was brutally murdered in a killing spree that lasted three months and claimed the lives of nearly a million Rwandans.

How could anybody survive such an ordeal?

Embracing the Journey of Recovery

Incredibly, Immaculee survived the slaughter. For 91 days, she and seven other women huddled together in a local pastor's cramped bathroom while hundreds of machete-wielding killers hunted them.

How could anybody even consider forgiving the people who had brutally murdered her family? Yet this is exactly what happened.

During those endless hours of unspeakable terror, Immaculee discovered the power of prayer. She eventually faced her fear of death and developed a profound and lasting relationship with God. She emerged from her hideout having discovered the meaning of truly unconditional love—a love so strong she was able to seek out and forgive her family's killers.

On PBS TV, Immaculee Ilibagiza appeared with internationally renowned author and speaker Dr. Wayne Dyer.

She has authored a book called "Left to Tell."

"Left to Tell" is Immaculee's triumphant story of her journey through the darkness of genocide. It will inspire anyone whose life has been touched by fear, suffering and loss. We can all learn the incredible power of prayer and the power of forgiveness from this remarkable young woman.

THE POWER OF RITUALS AND TRADITIONS

Joan was brought up in a strict Roman Catholic family. She had a strong faith in God even though she disagreed with the church's views on abortion and divorce. In her deepest and darkest moment of despair Joan decided that God would look after her and she began to ask the members of her congregation for support. She thoroughly enjoyed the formal rituals and services where prayer and giving thanks is of paramount importance.

The advantage of churches, synagogues and organized groups is that there is strength in numbers. If you are going through a particularly rough time spiritually, emotionally and/or physically, it is essential to have the support of like minded individuals. There are many proponents for and opponents against organized religion — but you really need to find out for yourself and see if this works for you.

There is a story of one young man who visited a local parish and it seems that he was not impressed with the church or the priest. As he was leaving the church, the priest was anxious to meet his new guest and asked him if he enjoyed the service and if he would visit them again. "I don't think so," exclaimed the young man. "You're all a bunch of hypocrites."

The priest calmly retorted. "Yes, but we always have room for one more!"

There are many proponents who do not believe that the type of group is important. However, the power of the group is invaluable — successful people are rarely lone rangers.

This leads us into the next crucial element in the process of recovery—Support Groups.

SUPPORT GROUPS

Thankfully we don't have to reinvent the wheel!

Embracing the Journey of Recovery

There are support groups for practically every ailment, malady and affliction known to mankind. There are support groups for cancer, diabetes, fibromyalgia, battered women, overeaters, alcoholics, drug addicts, sex addicts, victims of violence and victims of sexual abuse. The most widely used is the 12 step program originated by Alcoholics Anonymous in 1935 and this philosophy has been successfully used by dozens of other support groups. They can range in quality from being very helpful to being not helpful at all. Ask your health professional, spiritual advisor, family members or friends if they know of any support group for your particular condition.

HEALTH PROFESSIONALS

Your health professionals and you are responsible for determining the best possible course of action for looking after your particular health challenge. It is truly a partnership and it is always a two way street. Joan had several professionals involved in the treatment of and her recovery from breast cancer. She utilized the services of a primary care physician, oncologist, radiation oncologist, surgeon, naturopath, and spiritual advisor.

Joan's breast cancer was very aggressive and required immediate intervention.

Initially, Joan was against all the invasive and drastic procedures but without it she would most likely have died. She would have preferred to go through life using only natural health care from her naturopathic physician and support from her church group. The good news was that after her surgery and chemotherapy, she was able to utilize her natural healing approach. She needed every single possible resource to recover and it was still a very slow, agonizing return to health.

In many cases you do not have a choice in choosing your health care provider. However, you always have a choice in saying yes or no to their proposed treatment plan. You are not limited to one health professional. Progressive health professionals encourage a multi-disciplinary approach to healing. They recognize that they are experts in their field but in many cases a patient requires other forms of therapy as well. If at all possible, try and align yourself with a health professional who not only excels in their given field but also has your health and well being as their number one priority. With your best interests at heart, he will consider alternate and complementary treatment options.

BARING YOUR SOUL AND BEING EMOTIONALLY NAKED

Whether you are recovering from chemical dependency, cancer, depression or a severe motor vehicle accident, sooner or later you have to bare your soul to at least one other person. "A problem shared is a problem cut in half." The act of releasing the pain, anguish, guilt and the "why me" attitude produces results beyond belief. Confession has been around for centuries for a very good reason. It works.

Step 5 of Alcoholics Anonymous states that we "admitted to ourselves to God and to another human being the exact nature of our wrongs". The challenge for most people undertaking a heart to heart talk is the issue of trust. AA recommends a priest, pastor or someone who is non judgmental and completely trustworthy; usually a professional. The whole idea is for the person to unburden themselves.

QUESTIONS TO ASK AND POINTS TO PONDER

Who else has been through what you are going through?

Remember that you don't have to reinvent the wheel. In your circle of family, friends, and even enemies, somebody has been through what you have been through. The key is to ask for help! There will always be somebody out there willing to help you. However, they will not be able to help you if they do not know you are hurting.

Ask your family and friends about finding a support group, mentor, sponsor or spiritual advisor.

If you are truly sincere, you will find these resources easily. Who is your support network? Make phone calls, visit the library and use the computer and then ask your family and friends for help.

READ STORIES OF TRIUMPHS OVER ADVERSITY

My vote for the greatest Canadian of all time was an easy choice. I chose the incredible Terry Fox. Terry was a very physically active young man who suffered a severe form of cancer. He had his leg amputated but was very determined to find a cure for cancer. He had the audacity to say he was going to run across Canada with his one leg and his artificial prosthesis to raise money for the cure of cancer. Terry utilized all of the resources that we have discussed. He had strong faith, an absolutely huge support network and most of all he believed he was going to succeed. He also had quite a sense of humor.

"I bet some of you feel sorry for me. Well don't. Having an artificial leg has its advantages. I've broken my right knee many times and it doesn't hurt a bit."

Even with his courageous effort, Terry succumbed to the disease and was forced to stop his Marathon of Hope in 1980. He died on June 28, 1981 but the spirit of Terry Fox is still alive and well and as strong as ever. Each year across Canada and several other countries there are Terry Fox Runs. His dream, carried forward by his friends, families and supporters has raised over 25 million dollars to date.

If you are recovering from a life threatening condition or severe injury and disability, find a person who can be your inspiration, role model and hero. Terry's Marathon of Hope brings happy tears to me when I am feeling discouraged, distraught or sad. I can push harder and go one step further when I think of his heroic efforts. Each time I am running a marathon (26.2 miles) and feel pain, I remember that Terry ran a marathon a day for consecutive weeks.

CHAPTER SUMMARY

1. The first step on the road to recovery from a life threatening disease or illness is to find a higher power. It does not matter who or what the higher power is. It is only important that you have one.

2. It is crucial to find a support group, and work hand in hand with your health professionals to formulate a game plan.

3. It is absolutely crucial to bare your soul to a trusted individual and unburden yourself from your current pain, past sins or future anxiety.

4. Knowledge is power. Look for personal stories of recovery at the library or on the internet. If these people can recover, so can you!

The message of Chapter One is the message of Hope. Remember the horrible tragedy of the tsunami in Indonesia on Boxing Day of 2004? For those who survived the devastating tsunami and lost everything including their families, jobs and all their worldly possessions, it is amazing that they have made it this far. *Thailand and its neighboring countries have changed from a "disaster area" to a "construction area."* There is much work to be done — but a journey of 1000 miles begins with one small step. They have taken a huge step so far! Remember, if you tap into your higher power, you also tap into the immense powers of the universe.

Now that we have been given the message of Hope; what next?

The next chapter explores the realms of our higher purpose. Who are we living for? What are we living for? Get ready for the next step of the journey.

RESOURCES

1. Scrivener, Leslie (2000). *Terry Fox: His Story*. (2000). Toronto: McClelland and Stewart.

2. Dossey, Larry, *Prayer is Good Medicine* (1996). Canada: Harper Collins.

3. *Alcoholics Anonymous: The Big Book Online* http://www.aa.org/bigbookonline/

What is Your Higher Purpose?

What is Your Higher Purpose?

In Chapter One, we discussed the importance of a faith in a higher power. If we can make it through difficult times with the help of a power greater than ourselves, we can live a worthwhile and meaningful life.

I have three personal questions to ask:

1. **What are you living for?**

Is there a huge burning desire to climb Mount Everest when you get healthy? Or is it something much simpler such as walking down the street pain free?

2. **What is at the end of your rainbow?**

If you are going to go through the long, bumpy and sometimes agonizing road of recovery, there's got to be a pot of gold at the end of the rainbow! (Or at least a bowl of ice cream.)

3. What activities do you miss the most?

I frequently ask my practice members what activities they miss the most because of their ailments.

The answers are very diverse and include such responses as:

- I miss being able to pick up my grand kids.

- I would love to be able to play a round of golf again.

- If only I could sleep through the night without being awakened by pain.

- All I want to do is to be able to work.

- If I get better, I am going to take my wife on a trip around the world.

- There has to be huge internal motivation to get up and get going each day. What is it for you?

After the first few weeks of treatment, Donny began to discuss his plans for the future with his peers. He loved working with people in his profession and he also loved playing sports. Although many of his peers claimed he had too lofty ambitions, Donny definitely knew what he wanted to do when he got better. He had a definite purpose for his life once he regained his health.

MAN'S SEARCH FOR MEANING

In "Man's Search for Meaning", Viktor Frankl described the absolute horrors and atrocities of living as a prisoner in a Nazi concentration camp. He was a doctor and observed first hand the suffering and death of hundreds of fellow prisoners. Dr. Frankl's horrific descriptions of the forced labor camps, torture and starvation are absolutely frightening. Yet some people managed to survive the ordeal because they had something extraordinarily special to live for. At each moment, they had a higher purpose in their life.

I would highly recommend "Man's Search for Meaning" for its profound and sobering analysis of a very important subject. How can human beings survive and transcend such horror and cruelty?

I have included a few quotes from Dr. Frankel's book* for your perusal.

"What matters, therefore, is not the meaning of life in general, but rather the specific meaning of a person's life at a given moment." p.171

"Everything can be taken from a man but ...the last of the human freedoms—to choose one's attitude in any given set of circumstances, to choose one's own way." p.104

"A man who becomes conscious of the responsibility he bears toward a human being who affectionately waits for him, or to an unfinished work, will never be able to throw away his life. He knows the "why" for his existence, and will be able to bear almost any 'how'." p.127

The key phrase I find most fascinating is that if man knows the "why" for his existence he will be able to bear almost any "how".

Why are you willing to fight so hard to not only survive but to thrive?

---

* Above quotations reprinted from: Frankl, Viktor E., **Man's Search for Meaning**, Washington Square Press, Simon and Schuster, New York, 1963.

Embracing the Journey of Recovery

The statement above applies not only to the survivors of Nazi Concentration camps, but also to anybody undergoing extreme hardship and adversity today.

To **Viktor Frankl**, meaning is experiencing by responding to the demands of the situation at hand, discovering and committing oneself to one's own unique task in life, and by allowing oneself to experience or trust in an ultimate meaning - which one may or may not call God.

Donny remembered reading Viktor Frankl's book and quickly realized that his life was not so bad after all. He had food, shelter, family and friends—furthermore, he did not have a gun pointed at his head forcing him to work so he could live another day!

What do you think about when you are going through tough times?

HOW WOULD YOUR HERO OR ROLE MODEL ACT IN A SIMILAR SITUATION?

When one is going through extreme hardships, it is often helpful to ask the following question. "What would my hero do if this happened to him/her?"

Joan began attending a woman's support group at her church after she was released from the hospital. In one of the group sessions, Joan explained in painful detail how awful and despondent she felt. During the group session, her friend Genevieve then asked her two insightful and thought-provoking questions.

"Do you have a hero Joan?"

"Of course I do. Most of you know that my hero is Roberta Bondar."

Dr. Roberta Bondar was one of the first six Canadians chosen for astronaut training in 1983. She was also fortunate enough to be chosen to fly in the space shuttle Discovery in January, 1992. Roberta is not just an astronaut but also a physicist, a scientist and a photographer.

Joan had extreme admiration for Roberta and kept a scrapbook of her fascinating career.

Genevieve asked Joan another pointed question. "What do you think Roberta would do if she were recovering from breast cancer?"

Joan burst into tears for several minutes and then suddenly began laughing.

"Roberta wouldn't be focusing on what's wrong with life — like I am. She wouldn't be focusing on all the pain and darkness. Instead, she'd concentrate on the beauty and what's great about life."

Joan had actually met Roberta and listened to her describe her experiences of photographing the beauty of the earth from outer space and "back on earth". In fact, one of Dr. Bondar's projects had been photographing the National Parks of Canada.

In a conversation with Joan, Roberta talked about pulling herself out of deep, dark feelings of loneliness and despair by reminding her that beauty was always there at the same time. She has pulled out of her sadness and low ebb times by remembering the beauty on earth — and thousands of miles above it.

"That's what I am going to do!" Joan exclaimed.

Embracing the Journey of Recovery

"I'm going to remember all the beauty and love and happiness that I have in my life. I don't feel very beautiful right now, walking around with a bald head and no tits. But I can certainly feel the beauty, care, love and warmth of this group. It's going to be a tough road ahead, but I think I can do it. Thank you so much for being here for me. You guys truly are beautiful!"

By answering a simple but powerful question from her friend, Joan began to embrace the journey of recovery. Support groups are crucial in the recovery from any life threatening condition. However, each individual must challenge themselves by fully participating in the recovery program. Recovery is not a spectator sport and feelings of sadness, anger and shame are a natural and necessary part of the process. Asking for help from one's support group is absolutely indispensable.

Asking for help from their individual support groups allowed both Joan and Donny to move forward on their respective journeys of recovery.

If you or your loved one is stuck and floundering while recovering from a life threatening ordeal, ask the thought provoking question, "What would my hero do if s/he were in my shoes?"

It is very important to draw upon the strength of one's higher power but why not draw upon the strength of your hero as well?

CHAPTER SUMMARY

The simplest and fastest way to move ahead in one's recovery is to define one's higher purpose.

What are you focused on?

Is your ultimate purpose in life more important than your current struggle?

Remember Donny's epiphany of recalling the deep truths revealed by Victor Frankl.

"A man who becomes conscious of the responsibility he bears toward a human being who affectionately waits for him, or to an unfinished work, will never be able to throw away his life. He knows the 'why' for his existence, and will be able to bear almost any 'how'".

Also remember Joan's shift from darkness and gloom to beauty and joy by remembering her hero Roberta Bondar and how she would handle her dilemma.

If you have a higher power and a higher purpose, the next step is to develop an attitude of gratitude.

Get ready for the next chapter. The journey is going to become even more incredible.

Embracing the Journey of Recovery

EXERCISES

Take out a pen and paper and write down your answers to the following questions:

1. What is your higher purpose?

2. What or who are you living for?

3. What would your hero or role model do if s/he had your condition?

How to Develop an Attitude of Gratitude

How to Develop an Attitude of Gratitude

"Learn to get in touch with the silence within yourself, and know that everything in life has purpose. There are no mistakes, no coincidences, all events are blessings given to us to learn from"

Elizabeth Kubler-Ross

THE ROLLER COASTER RIDE

Donny was having a rollercoaster ride in treatment. Some days he felt as high as a kite and other days he felt as low as the bottom of the ocean. To Donny's surprise, the counselors told him that ups and downs were a normal and expected part of recovery.

One day after a particularly draining group session, Donny's friend Mel unloaded on him. In 10 minutes, Mel had described in agonizing detail everything that was wrong with his life. He was going through a painful divorce, had defaulted his home mortgage and his job was in jeopardy. Donny had finally heard enough and told Mel to calm down and stop his "whine" fest.

"Yes, you've got problems Mel, but there must be something good happening in your life. Before you say another word, I want you to take this sheet of paper and write at least 10 things in your life that you are grateful for", said Donny.

"I'll help you get started. Number one is that you have a wonderful daughter who absolutely adores you," said Donny.

Mel was stunned by Donny's words, but quickly took his sheet of paper and came up with 10 things he was grateful for.

- My daughter Jade

- My Mom and Dad

- My peers here at the treatment centre

- My beautiful home

- My great job (If I clean up, I may still have a great job to go back to)

- My dog

- My treatment counselor Brian

- My ability to help other people with their problems

- The opportunity to finally begin to face my problems

- I'm beginning to feel healthy for the first time in 20 years

Wow! Needless to say, Mel had an absolute attitude transformation in five minutes! He had quickly shifted from self pity and self loathing to gratitude and acceptance.

Chapter 3

COUNT YOUR BLESSINGS

One of my favorite books of all time is *Count Your Blessings: The Healing Power of Gratitude and Love*, by Dr. John F. Demartini.

I firmly believe Dr. Demartini when he states that "All complete healing is activated through love and gratitude...

Few situations urge us to examine our life more than the possibility of our own impending death...

For many people, including our loved ones, the day they are diagnosed with a life threatening illness is the day they truly begin to live and appreciate life."

In "Count Your Blessings", Dr. Demartini talks about balancing perceptions. In many instances our reality of a situation is not nearly as good or as bad as we think it is. It all depends upon one's perspective.

In the following story, we can see how reality and perspective can change very quickly.

There is a very old Sufi story about a man whose son captured a strong, beautiful, wild horse, and all the neighbors told the man how fortunate he was. The man patiently replied, "We will see." One day the horse threw the son who broke his leg, and all the neighbors told the man how cursed he was that the son had ever found the horse. Again the man answered, "We will see." Soon after the son broke his leg, soldiers came to the village and took away all the able-bodied young men, but the son was spared. When the man's friends told him how lucky the broken leg was, the man would only say, "We will see." Gratitude for participating in the mystery of life is like this.

Embracing the Journey of Recovery

The same principle applies to people such as Donny, Mel and Joan. In Mel's case, he was totally focused on all his problems when in reality; he had just as many good things happening in his life. However, it takes patience and training to develop an attitude of gratitude. It is very easy to be grateful when things are going your way. It is not so easy to have gratitude when you are in pain, suffering or grieving a loss.

The key to developing an attitude of gratitude is to practice it every day. At the end of each day, take inventory. Do not ignore or deny the events or situations that are painful but acknowledge them. At the same time, acknowledge the good things that happened to you. Nobody is asking you to pretend or deny that you are having serious difficulties. Simply understand the simple truth that in each and every day there are plenty of things to be grateful for. It is virtually impossible for a person to heal and become well if they are 100% focused on pain and suffering.

In the early days of Donny's recovery at the treatment centre, he was so sick that he could barely walk. He had lost control of his bladder and many people made fun of him. He was detoxifying from the alcohol and drugs and experiencing severe withdrawal symptoms such as hallucinations and shaking. He did not know if he was going to live and he felt humiliated that others were laughing at him.

Even in his severely weakened state, the counselors made him find one good thing that happened to him on each day. What good could he possibly find on any day since entering treatment?

Suddenly, he remembered the kindness of one of his peers. Shawna had seen the others making fun of him and befriended him. She was very kind to Donny because the same thing had happened to her when she was "detoxing".

She told Donny what she had been through and emphatically told him he was in the right place and that he would get better. This act of kindness was the flicker of light and hope that kept Donny trying for just another day.

A similar incident happened with Joan. After she had her surgery, she found herself to be physically unattractive and wretched. Joan felt very insecure and feared physical rejection from her husband. However, the nurse came to her door and said she had a visitor. It was her husband Jackie.

Jackie and Joan faced each other and felt very awkward for several minutes. Joan was so emotional that she could not utter a word. Jackie finally broke the ice by telling Joan, "I love you very much and no matter what happens, I am going to support you all the way —I know you feel horrible — but somehow, someway we are going to get you through it".

Joan was so grateful and from that moment on began to experience the feeling of hope.

Possessing an attitude of gratitude is absolutely essential to recovering from a life threatening illness or injury. It does not matter what has happened to you, it only matters what you are going to do about it. Developing an attitude of gratitude is a pillar in embracing the process of recovery.

Embracing the Journey of Recovery

EXERCISES

1. Take time in the evening to reflect upon what has happened to you during the last 24 hours. Acknowledge each event and then write down at least 10 things that you are grateful for. Do this every day until it becomes automatic.

2. Can you remember a day when absolutely everything went wrong? Write down at least five things that you could be grateful for on that particular day. This is a very difficult exercise but it will help you immensely in your recovery.

3. Each morning say the following: "Something wonderful is going to happen to me today." If you practice this affirmation for 30 days in a row you will start to recognize and appreciate a multitude of wonderful events.

4. Has there been anything in your life that seemed like a great misfortune at the time, but turned out to be a blessing in disguise?

Developing an attitude of gratitude is vital in helping you cope with relentless and unbearable pain.

But why does pain have to hurt so much?

It's onward to the next chapter to find out.

Chapter 4

Overcoming the Pain
Barrier

Overcoming the Pain Barrier

"DOC, WHY DOES PAIN HAVE TO HURT SO MUCH?"

As Joan was recovering from her surgery, she was also undergoing tests to determine if her body was cancer free. She felt somewhat stronger physically but her self confidence was still extremely low. She longed to be back at work and helping other people recover from their illnesses. Then she suddenly remembered a very profound conversation she had with one of her patients a few years back. The patient's name was Francis and he had suffered a near fatal accident while surfing the big waves in Hawaii. Unfortunately, Francis had suffered a very serious spinal cord injury. He had no feeling in his legs for a long time and then he gradually started to get his feeling back. It first started as a small tingle and then it progressed to a pulsing sensation. Finally, months later, he experienced excruciating pain. The pain was so strong and unbearable that he alternated between screaming and crying. The pain became so intense that one day Francis asked the attending doctor, "Doc, why does pain have to hurt so much? Why am I getting worse?"

I have heard these questions on numerous occasions and I have attempted to answer them in several different ways. The best explanation I have heard in describing pain comes from my colleague Dr. Barry Weinberg.

PAIN IS SEPARATION

"Pain is nothing more than the experience of separation. If you cut your finger with a knife, the separation of the skin causes pain. If you break a bone, the separation of the bone tissue causes pain. If you break up a relationship or a loved one dies, the separation from that person causes emotional pain. All pain is separation.

"If the separation continues and becomes great enough, the pain begins to diminish until it is no longer felt. In these circumstances we may feel the injury or trauma is "healing", because the pain is going away. In fact, the pain is diminishing because the separation is becoming so great that it grows beyond our level of awareness. Rather than healing (becoming whole) we are merely becoming numb."

In the case of Francis, the injury to his spinal cord had caused 100% separation between the spinal cord and his legs. He could not feel anything and his legs were totally useless. He was paralyzed. Through extensive physical rehabilitation, Francis was fortunate enough to have the nerve flow restored between his spinal cord and his legs. To feel pain is far better than to feel nothing.

WHY DOES IT HURT WHEN YOU BEGIN TO HEAL?

Dr. Barry further explains why your body hurts more when you begin to heal.

"There are two reasons. One, as you heal, or become more whole, you become more aware of your body and yourself. With this increased aware-ness, the pain signals are experienced more. It is not that the pain is get-ting "worse"... you are feeling more. Healing is not about feeling better; it is about being better able to feel.

"The more aware we are of the subtle signals of our bodies, minds and spirits, the more able we are to adapt to the changes in our environment. Would you rather hear the lion's roar miles away...or feel its breath on your neck? When we are more aware of the subtle, we have more room to make decisions. Our bodies give us such signals, but often they are ignored. Over time, the body must get our attention or more severe circumstances will ensue. We begin to experience pain...if we don't listen to this more advanced signal, the pain will increase to a point, but then suddenly stop. We have become numb. This part of us will surely die, unless immediate and critical action is taken. As that part, which has become so separate that it is unfelt, begins to become more whole with the body, the pain will return. Often it will be very intense, but as the healing continues it reduces and we begin to enjoy a finer quality of life. In order to heal, that part must be felt. We must be aware of it."

Joan recalls the days of agony for Francis very clearly. However, she also recalls his determination to persist though the pain and religious-ly perform his rehabilitation exercises daily. He had a strong belief in God even though he sometimes thought that for some strange reason

God was punishing him. He also had a strong desire to once again be a provider for his partner and two children. His love for them and to be with them was his higher purpose in life. But, most of all he was very grateful just to have the opportunity to recover.

ONE OF JOAN'S HAPPIEST DAYS

One of the happiest moments in Joan's career was to see Francis walk from one end of the room to the other. In a profoundly spiritual experience, Francis, his family and Joan burst into tears simultaneously. These happy tears represented the awesome healing power of gratitude and love.

A few weeks later, Joan asked Francis if all the pain and utter turmoil was worth it. He said he would gladly go through the experience twice over just to be able to experience walking again.

After recalling the courage of Francis, Joan immediately decided that she could be just as strong as he was and persist and push forward even in the face of seemingly insurmountable obstacles. Joan was once again embracing her journey of recovery.

CHAPTER SUMMARY

Pain is caused by separation. As you heal and become more whole, you become more aware of your body and yourself. With this increased awareness in your mind, body and spirit, the pain signals are experienced more. Remember that the pain is not necessarily getting "worse" but more likely that you are you are just feeling more. "Healing is not about feeling better; it is about being better able to feel."

EXERCISES:

1. Who do you know who has recovered from a life threatening illness or injury? Seek them out and ask them how they did it. It is very likely that that you have several fascinating people in your own community with remarkable stories of recovery.

2. Celebrate your victories even if they are small ones. Examples include:

    *   I am now 30 days clean and sober.

    *   I have been pain free for a whole day.

    *   I slept through the night with no pain.

In the next chapter, we are going to experience a health professional's return to work while he was still wounded.

Read the next chapter and learn the secrets of flourishing as a wounded healer.

The Power of the Wounded Healer

Chapter 5

The Power of the Wounded Healer

"The Doctor is effective only when he himself is affected. Only the wounded physician heals. But, when the doctor wears his personality like a coat of armor, he has no effect."

(Carl Jung: *Wounded healer of the Soul*)

The concept of working while recovering was not new to Donny as he had read Henri Nouwen's enlightening book entitled *The Wounded Healer*. Donny had received counseling from Reverend Alice in addition to his ongoing care from the treatment centre. She asked him to read the book because she felt Donny could still be effective as a member of his healing profession while he was working through his own recovery process. The book was written primarily for ministers who wanted to be of service in their community, but Reverend Alice thought the concepts could also be used by Donny in his current situation.

Embracing the Journey of Recovery

IS THERE SUCH A WORD AS WOUNDEDNESS?

The Wounded Healer is a hope-filled and profoundly simple book that speaks directly to those men and women who want to be of service in their church or community. According to Nouwen, ministers [or members of the healing professions] are called to identify the suffering in their own hearts and make that the starting point of their service.

Nouwen speaks about the fundamental "woundedness" in human nature. This "woundedness" can serve as a source of strength and healing when helping others in the healing process. It is his contention that ministers are called to recognize the sufferings in their own hearts and make that recognition the starting point of their service.

After Donny had completed the first phase of his program at the treatment centre, he was allowed to work part time in his practice. He still had to eat, sleep and attend group sessions at the treatment centre and debrief with his counselors and peers each and every day. The counselors felt that Donny was not strong enough to go back to his practice full time but felt he was very capable of beginning a graduated return to work. Not only did Donny have the support of his counselors, but he also had the full support of his medical doctor, family and friends.

DONNY'S RETURN TO WORK

Donny was very anxious and felt totally humiliated when he returned to work. He was hypersensitive and feared that his patients would never respect him and may stop seeing him if they found out he had just returned from a drug and alcohol recovery centre. He was very vague in telling people how he was doing and why he had been away from work. He was also fearful that his office manager did not fully trust him, even though she fully supported him in his recovery.

Why would Donny feel this way?

Even in the 21st century, alcoholism and addiction are poorly understood. One camp sees addiction as a legitimate disease and the other sees it as a lack of willpower or a moral defect.

Alan Leshner, Ph.D., director of the National Institute on Drug Abuse (NIDA) says the stigma associated with alcohol and drug addiction is one of the biggest problems experts face. He further states that the public has little sympathy for addicts. Many of the public do not see addiction as a disease, but as a conscious choice driven by weakness of character and criminal self-indulgence. Some even view twelve-step groups as little more than religious cults. However, he adds that "whether you like the person or not, you've got to deal with [their problem] as an illness".

Steven Hyman, M.D., who directs the National Institute of Mental Health, compares the disease of addiction to heart disease, which may also necessitate major lifestyle changes. "Take heart patients. We don't blame them for having heart disease," he says, but we ask them to follow a certain diet, to exercise, to comply with medication regimes. So it is with the addicted person — we shouldn't blame them for the disease, but we should treat them as being responsible for their own recovery."

Recovering alcoholics and drug addicts face discrimination in employment and health care, due to the fact that many people in society still see addiction as a moral shortcoming instead of an illness.

Embracing the Journey of Recovery

Those in the addiction field want to educate the public about addiction to help remove this stigma.

Despite the uncertainty about the exact definition of addiction, one fact remains clear. Addiction is a real malady that poses real dangers to real people in the real world.

Donny wisely told only those he knew and trusted about his recovery from addiction. "I sometimes wish I had cancer then I could tell everybody."

Despite these unpleasant and uncomfortable feelings, Donny was able to connect with his patients on a very deep and meaningful level. Donny was able to connect with a woman who had recently lost her husband. He knew from his own experience that recovery from a life threatening disease or loss of a loved one is like riding a very treacherous rollercoaster. He simply spoke from his heart and asked her if she had a lot of up and down days. Once the connection was made, the journey of healing became more manageable.

With a great amount of support, Donny was learning first hand the power of becoming a wounded healer. His pain was omnipresent, but his desire to help others through their pain helped him overcome his own. In fact, he felt as if he was a better healer now than before.

Donny returned to work on a slow and gradual basis. He spent two months as an in-patient and another two months in extended care before finally being released. He did not return to work full time until nearly three months after he left the treatment centre. His physical activity was restricted and he usually felt exhausted after each day or half-day of work. The journey of recovery was very slow but he was managing to live productively one day at a time.

CHAPTER SUMMARY

1. Recovering people are capable of helping others despite being wounded themselves. You can recognize the suffering in your own heart and make that recognition the starting point of your service. One advantage to being wounded is that you can relate to others in a powerful way. You will be able to empathize with others and understand what they are going through. This enhanced awareness may also enable you to be a better problem solver and develop innovative solutions.

2. Working as a wounded healer must be done on a very slow and gradual basis. Work should always be accompanied by plenty of rest and must be carefully supervised by trained professionals.

3. Helping others while recovering from a life threatening injury or illness is an extremely valuable tool to have in your arsenal. However, it is imperative that your main priority is to look after your own needs first.

4. Addiction is just as much an illness as cancer or heart disease.

Chapter 6

The Magnitude of Visualization

The Magnitude of Visualization

One morning I was involved in a very interesting conversation with one of my patients. He informed me that he had undergone eye surgery but had a long way to go before he was totally recovered. He was having trouble walking and maintaining balance, because his vision was still impaired. He then made a very profound statement. "You know doc, if you have good vision — you can walk with confidence."

I thought about his comment and realized that it could be applied both literally and figuratively. In the practical literal sense, it is very difficult for any person to go from point A to point B if they can't see where they are going. How can you have any confidence or hope of arriving at your destination if you cannot see where you are going?

Embracing the Journey of Recovery

HAVING A CLEAR CUT VISION

Those recovering from a life threatening illness or injury need to have a clear cut vision of where they want to go. If you refer back to chapter two, you will recall the importance of having a higher purpose or meaning in life. It is imperative that you have a clear picture of where you want to go on your journey. If you do not have a clear picture of where you want to go, how will you know when you get there?

A hockey player recovering from cancer is going to have a strong and clear vision of returning for his first game. A grandmother recovering from Hodgkin's disease may have a clear picture of picking up her grandson again. The model of visualization should not however be limited only to the sense of sight.

CREATIVE VISUALIZATION

In her book "Creative Visualization", Shakti Gawain invites her readers to recall pleasant experiences that they have had in the past. They should involve good physical sensations such as eating a delicious meal, receiving a massage, swimming in cool water, or making love.

> *"Creative visualization refers to the way in which we communicate from our mind to our body... Creative visualization is the perfect tool for healing because it goes straight to the source of the problem—your own mental concepts and images. Begin to picture yourself and affirm to yourself that you are in perfect radiant health; see your problem as being completely healed and cured."*

Donny had a dynamic vision of both returning to work with his patients and crossing the finish line in record time at his next marathon. Joan had a clear vision of returning to work with vim, vigor and vitality. Even though her body was still weak, she had an image of doing her rounds in the hospital with confidence and poise.

Any person recovering from a life threatening illness should have an absolutely clear idea of what they are going to do **when** (not if) they return to good health.

Although the following story is not health related, it illustrates one man's vision and the incredible power of visualization.

VISUALIZATION CAN BUILD BRIDGES AND MOVE MOUNTAINS

Over 150 years ago, William Hamilton Merritt was a man who dreamed of building the first bridge over the Niagara River. Although he did not have an exact image of what the bridge would look like, he knew he was going to do it. (I believe he had several images in his mind.) There were many obstacles that he had to overcome before his dream came true. However, he focused on the completed project rather than on the obstacles.

His first objective was to create a line of communication – that was followed by a solid line to establish a link to the other side. The gorge was 800 feet wide and it was too dangerous to attempt this link by water. However, it occurred to somebody that kite-flying might be the answer to this difficult problem.

A contest was held offering a five dollar prize to the person who could fly a kite across the Niagara Gorge. A young American boy named Homan Walsh won the contest on the second day of the competition by flying his kite from the American shoreline to the Canadian shoreline. The string of his kite was fastened to a tree on the American shoreline and then a light cord was attached to it and pulled across. Next came a heavier cord, then a rope and finally a wire cable composed of several strands of number ten wire which formed the foundation of the new bridge.

Fifty foot wooden towers were erected on each bank and a wire cable 1,190 feet in length was passed over the top of the towers and anchored.

On July 26th, 1848, the first Niagara Suspension Bridge was completed.

This outstanding accomplishment started with a vision. William Hamilton Merritt focused on his dream of building the first bridge over the Niagara River. He overcame many obstacles because his focus was on the completed project.

For persons recovering from a life threatening illness or injury, it is absolutely imperative to keep focused on the completed project.

CHAPTER SUMMARY

1. "If you have good vision you can walk with confidence."

2. In the beginning, your vision of good health may be as weak as the kite string that flew across the Niagara River. Keep practicing and the image will progress to a light cord. The light cord will become a heavier cord, a rope, and finally a strong wire cable.

EXERCISES

I. Read the inspirational Bestseller **Creative Visualization** by Shakti Gawain. She is gifted in blending the rational approach of the western mind with the deep intuitive wisdom of the east.

If you have made an honest and willing attempt to do the exercises at the end of each chapter, you will already be experiencing profound changes in your life. However, the best is yet to come. Chapter 7 examines the great potential that can be realized by helping yourself or helping others.

How to Help Yourself and Help Others

How to Help Yourself and Help Others

At some point along the journey of recovery, there is one crucial question that needs to be answered:

What is the focal point in my recovery?

Should I put 100% of my energy **into helping myself**?

Or, should I have a more balanced approach and spend some of my time <u>helping others</u>?

YIN AND YANG

Let's consider the concept of the Chinese philosophy known as yin and yang and analyze the possibilities.

The yin and the yang are two fundamental principles. One negative, dark, passive, cold, wet, and feminine (yin) and the other positive, bright, active, dry, hot and masculine (yang). The interactions and balance of these forces in people and nature influence their behavior and fate.

A person recovering from a severe illness such as cancer may ask the following questions:

Is it not my responsibility to do whatever it takes to recover from my illness? What is wrong with being a little selfish for a change? What is wrong with spending all my energy on getting **me** healthy? I can help other people later.

However, many health professionals and persons in active recovery also recognize the importance of working with others. If you are solely focused on your problems, your life becomes one-dimensional and unbalanced. Isn't healing about balance? Isn't it about giving and receiving?

In Joan's case, the main focus of her life was looking after others. She worked all day helping her patients recover from their illnesses and then came home and put on her mother and wife hat. Although she loved her family very much, the fact of the matter was she did most of the giving most of the time.

I am certain that many readers can relate to Joan's story. However, there does come a time and a place where being "selfish" (as opposed to self-centered) is absolutely essential for one's recovery.

My practice members frequently express their absolute devotion in fulfilling the needs of their children. I entirely agree that children's needs have to be satisfied since they have not yet learned how to look after themselves.

However, I invite the reader to consider the following story about constantly putting the needs of children first.

SHOULD THE CABIN PRESSURE DROP...?

When traveling on any major airline, passengers are required to listen to a mandatory presentation on safety procedures. The flight attendants politely (and with big smiles) discuss the safety features of the aircraft; emergency exits and the proper procedure for correctly fastening seat belts.

"Should the cabin pressure drop, it may become difficult to breathe and oxygen masks will immediately drop down from the overhead bins. (*The next sentence is crucial.*)

If you are traveling with small children; put your mask on first to begin breathing and then put the masks on your children.

You come first! Not the child! If you do not put your mask on first, both you and your child may die!

The message is that there may be a time and situation when the needs of the parent come before the needs of the child.

It did not take Joan too long before she realized that her successful recovery depended upon putting herself first. The needs of others would have to be put on hold.

DONNY CHOSE TO HELP OTHERS

Donny's story was somewhat different. Although he was totally devoted to looking after his patients all day long, he did not have any dependents to support at home. In the early months of his recovery, he lived on his own with no significant other or children.

After he was about six months clean and sober, Donny was encouraged by his sponsor and his peers to begin helping others. By doing service and volunteer work, he would not only be helping others but he would also be helping his own recovery. Donny took his assignment seriously and regularly became the chairman for his AA home group.

THE HARSH AND COLD REALITY OF ALCOHOLISM

Donny was also was privileged to lead an AA meeting at a local "detoxification" facility on three different occasions. The meetings at the detox facility kept Donny in touch with the physical pain, emotional anguish and feeling of hopelessness of those suffering from addiction. He gave a very simple message to those residents who attended the meetings. He told them that he had experienced the same thing that they were going through— he understood their pain and was there to give them hope. "If I can recover, so can you."

After approximately one year of sobriety, Donny had a day he would always remember. He had signed up with another AA member to lead an AA meeting at the local prison. The cold hard realty of alcoholism really hit home that night. The prison guards graciously welcomed Donny and his friend Pat and said most of the inmates were in prison because of crimes related to alcohol and drugs. The meeting went very well even though there only five people in attendance. One man described his problems with alcohol and how he had committed several break-ins and robberies to feed his habit. Donny sincerely believed that this man meant business and offered to take him to meetings after he was released.

After the meeting, Pat had two sobering things to tell Donny. First, he told Donny that he should not get his hopes too high, because many inmates were at a very high risk to relapse and to re-offend once released from prison.

Secondly, Pat also had some very bad news about one of Donny's peers, Bob, from the treatment centre. The disease had proven to be too much for Bob and he had tragically committed suicide. The news was devastating to Donny because he admired Bob's courage and determination. How could this possibly happen when Bob seemed to be doing so well?

Three weeks after the prison AA meeting, Donny received some more bad news from Pat. The man who expressed a great desire to clean up and go to AA after he got out of prison was once again in trouble with the law. Apparently, the same night he was released from prison, he got drunk, committed another robbery and was arrested. He was once again in prison!

Donny was learning the harsh and cold reality of alcoholism. The disease was deadly and progressive and countless people ended up either "locked up" or "covered up."

THE BIG BOOK'S PROMISES

However, with support from his sponsors and peers, Donny persevered and eventually experienced the joy of helping another person find and embrace the journey of recovery.

Embracing the Journey of Recovery

The gift for Donny in helping others was profound. He did not know it at the time, but he had begun to embrace the journey of recovery.

Others could see that Donny was progressing in his recovery because he had a **willingness to help others.** Some of the promises from the Big Book of Alcoholics Anonymous had come true. "Our whole attitude and outlook on life will change. We will lose interest in selfish things and gain interest in our fellows."

CHAPTER SUMMARY

Each story of recovery reflects an individual journey. Joan's situation was best suited for her to focus on herself and in a sense become "selfish." Donny's situation dictated that he spend some of his time helping others. By helping others he was also helping his own recovery.

EXERCISES

1. At this point in your recovery, is it in your best interest to look after yourself first before helping others?

2. If you are considering helping others and being a volunteer ask yourself the following questions:

What skills can I use in my current stage of recovery to help others? List at least four examples. (e.g. organizing events, helping children, cooking or driving)

Where would I like to volunteer? List three examples (e.g. Church, hospital or theatre.)

Who would I like to work with? (e.g.- with children, women or prisoners.)

Will helping others aid or hinder my recovery?

The next chapter examines the importance of the physical component of recovery.

Get ready for **The Fitness Prescription.**

The Fitness Prescription

The Fitness Prescription

What is the role of physical fitness in an individual's recovery program? It has been my experience that there is too much of a "cook book" approach in planning and implementing the physical component of the recovery process. Before embarking upon the physical component of any recovery program, it is absolutely imperative that the recovering individual obtain an accurate and comprehensive assessment of his current health status.

Some key questions that need to be addressed are:

- Is the individual capable and willing to begin a fitness program?

- What are the physical limitations of the individual?

- What is the ultimate goal for the individual's recovery? (To walk, to play the piano, to return to work)

- Which health professionals can help with the physical component of the recovery process?

- Who is the quarterback?

- How much supervision is required?

- What progress can be expected?

It is definitely beyond the scope of this book to discuss each and every aspect of a fitness program to help a person recover from a life threatening injury or illness. The thrust of this chapter is to discuss the possibilities, and available resources to get started.

THE FOUR KEY ELEMENTS IN DETERMINING A FITNESS PROGRAM

Although there are a multitude of factors to be considered in setting up an effective fitness program, I have condensed the vast amount of material down to four key elements.

1. Current Health Status

What is the current health status of the individual? How able are they to perform exercise? Do all the health professionals know the patient's limitations? A current, comprehensive and accurate medical report is indispensable and should be distributed to all the health professionals involved in the recovery program.

2. Realistic Long Term Goal(s)

What is the ultimate goal for the individual's recovery? Is there an anticipated date for return to work? What type of testing will be done to determine the individual's progress? Do the health professionals, family, support groups and recovering person all agree that this is a reasonable and achievable goal? It is crucial in this stage of the recovery progress to be both realistic and optimistic.

3. Incremental Short term Goals? (The Principle of Kaizen)

Kaizen means constant incremental improvement. Focusing on making small improvements day in and day out will allow you to reach your goals more quickly, easily and with less stress than any other method. Small incremental improvements seem inconsequential when viewed in the short term. However, small incremental improvements eventually pay very big dividends in the long term.

4. Utilizing a variety of Health Professionals and the Diverse Types of Therapy Available (What works for you?)

There are countless health professionals and various forms of therapy available to those who are recovering from a life threatening illness or injury. Ask for referrals from friends and family. What has worked for them? Remember that the treatment program is supposed to be coordinated and implemented by health professionals' not insurance companies.

   a. **Health Professionals:**
   - Medical Care
   - Chiropractic Care
   - Massage Therapy
   - Physical Therapy
   - Acupuncture
   - Naturopathy

- Herbalists
- Occupational Therapy
- Psychotherapy and Counseling
- Pastoral Counseling
- Nutritional Counseling
- Alternative Cancer therapies
- Holistic Healers
- Homeopathic Healing

b. **Alternate Types of Therapy:**

- Prayer and Meditation
- Laughter Therapy
- Light Therapy
- Aromatherapy
- Chelation
- Ayurveda
- Energy Healing
- Breathing Exercises
- Creative Visualization

DEVELOPING AN INDIVIDUALIZED FITNESS AND EXERCISE PROGRAM:

In an ideal world, the recovering individual will be evaluated by an exercise and fitness professional. Each individual has unique needs and requirements and it is essential that the program be appropriate to the individual at his or her current stage of recovery.

I am frequently asked the question, **"What is the best physical exercise to help me in my recovery?"** There is probably not one single activity or exercise that can cover all the bases. In order to develop an individualized fitness program, a fitness professional will consider the five components of fitness.

The generally accepted five components of fitness are:

I. Cardio-vascular endurance

- Common examples include swimming, biking or running.

2. Muscular strength

- Common examples include lifting weights or performing resistance exercises.

3. Muscular endurance

- Common exercises that will improve your muscle endurance include cardio-vascular activities such as walking, jogging, bicycling, or dancing.

4. Body composition

- Body composition refers to the relative amount of muscle and fat in a person's body. A person's total body weight (what you see on the bathroom scale) may not change over time — but the bathroom scale does not assess how much of that body weight is fat and how much is lean mass (muscle, bone, tendons, and ligaments). Body composition is important to consider for both health and weight management.

5. Flexibility

- Flexibility is the range of motion allowed by a joint and its surrounding musculature. Good flexibility in the joints can help prevent injuries through all stages of life. If you want to improve your flexibility, try activities that lengthen the muscles such as Yoga, Pilates or a basic stretching program.

A fitness professional will create a program which usually includes:

1. A variety of exercises including all five fitness components (e.g. walk, bike, stretch, yoga, etc.)

2. Appropriate frequency of exercise (Number of sessions per   week)

3. Proper intensity of the exercise (Mild, moderate, strenuous)

4. A combination of group exercise and one-on-one work.

5. Making the workouts both challenging and fun.

6. Contingencies for slow or no progress

7. A balance with other aspects of the recovery program.

8. Periodic progress reports.

9. Regular contact with all the other health professionals.

The program may not include all five fitness components due to physical limitations and considerations. However, a good fitness program will allow the individual to move forward and gain strength in his recovery. Getting started and moving forward are far more important than satisfying the requirements of a text book or an insurance company.

In this chapter, we will examine the Fitness Prescription for Joan and Donny once they were discharged from the hospital and the treatment centre.

It will become apparent to you that Donny's story and Joan's story are polar opposites.

DONNY'S STORY

Donny was a life-long athlete who loved to play sports. He played many team sports as a youngster including football, hockey and baseball. He was a competitive gymnast in his university days and until his disease took over he enjoyed competing in marathons and triathlons.

The Hotel California (Donny's nick-name for the treatment facility) only allowed Donny to go on 30 minute walks twice per day. The big treat was a one hour walk before lunch on Sunday. The challenge for Donny during his time as an in-patient, in extended care and after discharge was to keep his physical program in proper balance with the rest of his recovery.

In a nutshell, the doctor, counselor, peers and family members all agreed that Donny needed a balanced approach to his recovery. Donny needed to remember that exercise was only a part of the big picture.

Embracing the Journey of Recovery

AFTERCARE PROGRAM
(THE BIGGEST KEY TO HIS RECOVERY)

Donny and his peers were told that if they followed their after-care plan exactly as it was written, they would have a 100% chance of recovery.

An aftercare plan is a balanced approach to recovery and ensures that a recovering person stays on track. It is simple but requires self discipline and accountability for all actions taken or not taken.

Donny agreed to the following aftercare plan and with few variations follows it to this day. The key to any after care plan and any fitness program is self discipline.

"Self-discipline is the ability to make yourself do what you should do, when you should do it, whether you feel like it or not" ... (Elbert Hubbard)

Donny's After Care Plan

- I will attend three AA meetings per week
- I will attend after care group meetings each Tuesday
- I will talk to my sponsor weekly
- I will make three phone calls a week to recovery people
- I will eat three meals per day
- I will read the meditation book on a daily basis
- I will make my bed daily to remind me I'm in recovery
- I will exercise 3-4 times per week
- I will spend 20 minutes in meditation each day

Donny's Fitness Prescription

Donny's fitness prescription was very simple. He was allowed to run 30-45 minutes and stretch 3–4 times per week. He made sure he ate three meals per day, meditated 20 minutes daily and saw his chiropractor once per month. That's it. The key to his recovery was to put AA meetings and connecting to his recovery group first. This drove Donny crazy because he was used to working out intensely several times per week. However, he could negotiate an increase in the amount of his physical activity if he demonstrated that he was working an effective and balanced recovery program.

The message Donny learned was that physical fitness was only part of the total picture. His major focus was maintaining a balanced recovery program. If he adhered to a balanced program, everything else would fall in place easily.

JOAN'S STORY

At the best of times, Joan exercised sporadically. After being released from the hospital, she was physically weak and had very little motivation to do much of anything.

Whereas Donny had to be held back from exercising too much, Joan needed a big kick to get started.

Joan's recovery program differed from Donny's, but they both emphasized balance.

Joan agreed to the following recovery program:

- I will meet two times per week with my women's church group

Embracing the Journey of Recovery

- I will make daily phone calls to my family and friends

- I will continue to perform transcendental meditation twice daily for 20 minutes.

- I will walk five minutes twice a day (with help if necessary)

- I will eat three nutritious meals per day

- I agree to start a yoga class once I am physically stronger

- I will see a counselor every two weeks to help me with my recovery

- I will follow my doctor's orders and follow through with all necessary post-cancer tests and investigations

In the beginning, it took all of Joan's energy just to get through the day. She thoroughly enjoyed her women's group sessions but always felt exhausted afterwards. Her doctor insisted that she walk daily and told Joan to ask for support from her friends and family.

Her physical weakness combined with anger and depression was a big stumbling block. She constantly felt like giving up; and crying for long periods of time became a daily routine.

Joan's Fitness Prescription

Joan's progress was slow for many months following her surgery. Her doctor, women's group and counselor were all very concerned. They all agreed that Joan needed to get up, get out and start moving more.

A routine visit to the Doctor changed Joan's recovery permanently and in a very profound manner. Joan had never missed an appointment but she often had a negative attitude and complained of depression. Her doctor was a very compassionate man but always acted and dressed in a very professional manner. Joan was very depressed on this visit and had difficulty making eye contact. In fact, she was looking down at her doctor's feet when a big smile came across her face. She noticed that he was wearing a blue sock and a brown sock. To make things even funnier, she also noticed that the brown sock had a huge hole in it.

"Hey Doc, I notice you are wearing very religious socks today", chided Joan. "They're very holy!"

Her doctor immediately looked down at his socks and then turned beet red. They both looked at each other and simultaneously burst into thunderous laughter. Her doctor was embarrassed but could not stop laughing. More importantly, he noticed that Joan was full of energy and that her eyes became alive.

A DIFFERENT TYPE OF PRESCRIPTION

While they were both calming down from their fit of laughter, Joan's doctor started to write on his prescription pad. "Joan, I am writing out a different prescription for you today and I strongly urge you to take it seriously."

Much to Joan's surprise, she was prescribed a very powerful medicine that did not come in the form of a pill.

The prescription read:

Rx:

- Laugh 10 minutes per day
- Rent and watch one funny movie per week

- Repeat ad infinitum

Joan laughed through her tears when she read the prescription.

Later that day, Joan decided to start reading her husband's **Herman Cartoon Treasuries**. Joan's energy was drastically improved within a few weeks even though she still had bouts of depression. She started to walk on her own without coaxing and also organized weekly comedy movie nights at her house.

THE PHYSIOLOGICAL RESPONSES TO LAUGHING

For years afterwards, Joan claimed that one of the keys to her recovery was injecting humor and laughter into her life. Although it is not absolute science, studies have shown that stress hormones like adrenalin and cortisol are released when a person is stressed. These particular hormones may harm the body by suppressing the immune system and constricting the blood vessels. Researchers believe that laughing causes the body to release beneficial chemicals called endorphins which may counteract the effects of stress hormones and cause blood vessels to dilate and may also boost the immune system and reduce inflammation.

The endorphins released through Joan's daily laughter allowed her to get moving and was a great catalyst in her recovery. The action steps of walking with her support group plus daily laughter were Joan's fitness prescription. Joan had a new lease on life and was embracing her journey of recovery.

CHAPTER SUMMARY

Remember the four key components in determining a fitness program:

1. Current Health Status

2. Realistic Long Term Goal(s)

3. Incremental Short Term Goals (The Principle of Kaizen)

4. Utilize Your Health Professionals and the Diverse Types of Therapy Available (What works for you?)

Remember that your fitness program must be individualized to your current health status and to your goals.

Embracing the Journey of Recovery

EXERCISES

1. Find a fitness professional that is willing to work with you and your recovery team. Ask him/her to create an effective and individualized fitness program.

2. Make a written commitment to follow the program.

3. Create and follow an aftercare recovery program similar to Joan and Donny. Is the Fitness component in balance with rest of the program?

The Ultimate Test of Your Recovery Program

The Ultimate Test of Your Recovery Program

How does an individual truly know if his recovery program is working? As you are most likely aware, life does not necessarily follow what is taught in the classrooms or written in the text books. It is one thing to practice consistently, but what happens on game day is a true and more realistic measure of progress.

A true test of one's recovery from a life threatening injury or illness is to face yet another challenge or crisis.

DONNY'S CHALLENGE

For over a year, Donny conscientiously worked his recovery program to the best of his ability. He followed his after care plan 100% and had gradually returned to work on a full time basis. Under the close supervision of a counselor from the treatment centre, Donny was finally allowed to increase his physical training and compete in a marathon. He was ecstatic when he crossed the finish line in his fastest time ever. He worked hard at recovering financially and also began to rebuild his relationships with family and friends. Donny also began dating a woman and was both excited and scared about his new relationship. He had overcome many obstacles and was facing his challenges head on.

However, a 30 year old incident that had dramatically impacted his life was next on the horizon. This was to be a true test of his recovery program. Donny finally had an opportunity to go "toe-to-toe" with a demon from his past.

FACING THE DEMONS FROM THE PAST

Thirty years after the fact, the priest who had sexually assaulted Donny and several other young boys was finally being brought to justice. Donny was required to give evidence and undergo cross examination in both civil and criminal proceedings. Every detail of Donny's past would be scrutinized and he would be under extreme stress during the proceedings. His lawyer counseled him to tell the truth under all circumstances even if it was embarrassing and painful.

There were statements, affidavits, psychiatric examinations, conversations with the police and interest from the media. This case was huge and severely tested Donny's sobriety and recovery program. He used all of his support to help him thorough each day. He received tremendous support from his sponsor, his AA home group, the treatment centre, his office manager, his sister and especially from his new girlfriend.

After years of preliminary affidavits and court proceedings, Donny was faced with two crucial challenges. The first challenge was a civil cross examination by the lawyers representing the church and the priest. The result of which would be either a trial or (preferably) a judicially assisted dispute resolution. Secondly, there was a meeting with the crown prosecutor preparing him for the priest's upcoming trial.

Donny knew he had no control over the outcome but felt he had a responsibility to do his part to bring the priest to justice and to see church officials held accountable for their actions.

CIVIL PROCEEDINGS

The civil proceedings came first and Donny faced over six hours of cross examination from three different lawyers. He turned his will and his life over to his higher power to help him through this ordeal. His lawyer prepared him well and told him not to guess and not to get into arguments. He answered truthfully and with conviction and left the proceeding in a positive frame of mind. A few weeks later, both sides began preparing for a trial when the church officials contacted Donny's lawyer's office. The church lawyers had "blinked" and they were requesting a judicially assisted dispute resolution. Rather than face a media nightmare; the church wanted to come to a mutually acceptable solution.

Donny was allowed to express his concerns to the church officials and prepared a statement for this occasion. The two main points he raised in the Judicially Assisted Dispute Resolution were:

1. How the abuse affected his life and how the handling of the case by the church had severely exacerbated the situation.

2. To demonstrate the lack of accountability of the church towards him and the other victims/survivors.

After four hours of negotiating, the two sides finally came to an agreement. Although Donny was not allowed to talk about the terms of the agreement, he was very pleased that he and the others had finally convinced the church to become accountable and to issue a public apology.

A PUBLIC APOLOGY FROM THE CHURCH

The sense of relief was palpable to all who had been affected when they read in the church's national newspaper the apology from a high-ranking church official.

"On behalf of the whole church community, I want to publicly apologize to those persons - often family members, sometimes church members - who, when you tried to confront the church, were not heard or received in the way you needed to be. You were failed by our church and we are deeply sorry.

"On behalf of the whole church community, I want to publicly apologize to the families, partners and friends of these victims. You continue to be affected by and to struggle with the effect of the violence. You were failed by our church and for this we are deeply sorry."

By embracing the journey of recovery, Donny's feelings of anger and rage gradually began to dissipate. He truly hoped that the other survivors and their families were similarly able to begin their healing process.

Chapter 9

CRIMINAL COURT

The next issue to face was a meeting with the Crown Prosecutor. There were dozens of complaints against the former priest resulting in 20 official charges being laid from the Crown Prosecutor.

There had been many years of investigation and legal proceedings but the priest seemed to deny and minimize what he had done. Donny knew something big was happening when the crown prosecutor took a three hour airplane trip to meet him at the RCMP detachment of his home town. In a rather lengthy explanation, the crown prosecutor told Donny that the case had been settled and the priest had pleaded guilty to sexually assaulting three victims. He would be going to jail for at least four years. He and the other survivors would now have some form of closure. The ordeal was nearly over and all that remained was the sentencing. The highlights of the newspaper article read:

"Priest Gets Four Years for Assaults"

"An elderly former priest once thought of by his parishioners as "next to God" was led out of court in handcuffs yesterday to the applause of numerous former worshippers he had sexually assaulted. The priest bowed his head as he walked by a large throng of grim-faced victims and their families to begin serving a four-year prison sentence for abusing 10 young boys over a 22-year span. It was an emotional ending to a case that has gripped the church since it surfaced several years ago

"This sends a powerful message that sexual abuse of vulnerable children will not be tolerated in our society", said the Queen's Bench Justice who rejected the priest's request for a conditional sentence.

Embracing the Journey of Recovery

"This priest was the next thing to God Himself for a lot of people", said the Crown attorney who read out a series of heart-wrenching victim impact statements. "These people have shown a lot of courage in coming forward."

"A local victim's rights advocate said the priest is a "sexual psychopath" who deserved a prison sentence. Everything this man did was totally devoid of conscience", she said outside court.

"He is a very large man, a very imposing individual, and I picture him in those robes, just standing over those young children. It really sends chills up your spine."

With the tremendous support of his recovery group and the unwavering faith in his higher power, Donny was somehow able to survive this ordeal. His message at the dispute resolution still holds true today.

I have received an overwhelming response of caring, understanding and compassion from many wonderful people that I dared to trust with my story. I have emphatically faced each day with the purpose of conveying three important messages:

1. *Reach out and call a fellow AA member when you're in the middle of a crisis. Remember, all of our lives are important.*

2. *To the survivors, there is the message of hope. When you are ready to share the pain with a least one other caring person, the healing can begin.*

3. *To the abusers and those who cover up their dastardly actions, there are only two powerful and seemingly appropriate words. . .*

"God knows."

CHAPTER SUMMARY

1. There will always be challenges in life. Look at any challenge today from this day onward, and acknowledge the possibility that this apparent obstacle may be a gift sent to you by the universe.

"Learn to get in touch with the silence within yourself, and know that everything in life has purpose. There are no mistakes, no coincidences, all events are blessings given to us to learn from"

Elizabeth Kubler-Ross

2. There is no substitute for taking action on what needs to be done today. Taking action requires change, courage and determination. Donny felt the fear of change every step of the way but he always took action.

Embracing the Journey of Recovery

EXERCISES

1. What challenges, obstacles and pain are you facing right now? What action steps are you taking to move forward?

2. Where do you want to be six months from now? One year from now? Five years from now?

3. Ask for feedback from those closest to you. Do they see you moving forward in your recovery?

Embracing the Journey of Recovery

⬱

Embracing the Journey of Recovery

It is apparent from the preceding chapters that there are several key areas that need to be addressed when one is recovering from a life threatening injury or illness. At the <u>best</u> of times, recovery can be a heart-wrenching and unbearable ordeal for an individual and his supporters.

The first step on the journey of recovery is to properly assess the damage and get as accurate a diagnosis as humanly possible. Also, remember that the recovery of each individual involves the mind, body and spirit and one cannot function independently of the other. The mind, body and spirit are interconnected at all times.

The basic needs of the recovering individual include such factors as pain relief, support, motivation and a reason to recover. However, the number one ingredient for a successful recovery is to have hope. If you or your loved one is going through the most difficult and agonizing times of your life, remember just one thing. There is always hope.

I have shed many tears (both happy and sad) relating the stories of Joan and Donny to you, the reader. It is my hope that I have in some way reached your heart and given you hope to continue forward on your healing journey one day at a time.

Both Joan and Donny believed in, and had their own conception of God, (a.k.a. "A Higher Power"). They tapped into God in their own unique way and benefited from their faith in ways beyond understanding.

They also benefited from the power of their support groups and the guidance and coaching from their health professionals. The powerful message they learned was that they did not have to do it alone. Yes, each individual is 100% responsible for his/her own recovery and must take action every day. However, the magic and the joy of life come from our connectedness.

We all have our own individual journeys but some of my strongest and most meaningful experiences in life have come from being helped by a total stranger. Likewise, I have looked into the eyes of a stranger requiring first aid in an emergency situation and simply held their hand, looked into their eyes and told them that they were going to be okay. The feeling of being connected is from heart to heart. The key to recovery is opening up your heart. The big challenge is to open up your heart when you feel vulnerable, afraid, scared, and alone and in pain. To bare your soul and be emotionally naked with another human being requires absolute trust.

In the preceding chapters, there were some more difficult questions to ponder such as:

Chapter 10

What are you living for?

And…

What is your purpose in life?

Have you started to answer these questions yet?

Remember, if you are going to go through the long, bumpy and agonizing road of recovery, there's got to be a pot of gold at the end of the rainbow! (Or at least a bowl of ice cream.)

Another indispensable aspect of recovery is developing an attitude of gratitude by counting your blessings daily. Gratitude is not about seeing a "cruel" world through rose-colored glasses or hiding your head in the sand. It is about acceptance of your life on a daily basis. Each day there will continue to be tragedies, wars, disasters, pain and suffering. However, one can also find love, joy, peace, serenity and triumph over adversity on that same day. What can you be grateful for today? Write out your gratitude list now.

Overcoming the barrier of pain is another monumental obstacle to help us to recover from a life threatening injury or illness. Remember, Dr. Barry's incredible words of wisdom. "Pain is nothing more than the experience of separation."

If you cut your finger, break a bone or lose a loved one it is the separation that causes the pain. To experience agonizing and excruciating pain is undoubtedly one of the most difficult challenges we all face as human beings. Remember once more that you don't have to face the pain alone. Ask for help from your higher power and support group and keep focused on a positive outcome. Do you recall one of Joan's happiest days when she reflected upon her patient Francis? She asked him if all his pain and suffering was worth getting the use of his legs back. Francis said he would have experienced the pain twice over to experience walking again.

Donny's ability to access the power of the wounded healer was crucial for him in his recovery process. Under close supervision, it is possible to help others while you are healing yourself. Reverend Alice wisely told Donny to read the works of Henri Nouwen. Donny discovered that being wounded can serve as a source of strength and healing when helping others in the healing process. The key to harness the power is to recognize the suffering in one's own heart and make that recognition the starting point of their service to others.

In Donny's particular case, it was in his best interests to be helping others while he was healing himself. In Joan's case, her successful recovery was dependent upon putting her needs first. Do you recall the story of the airline safety announcement before each flight? Joan learned that she had to put on her oxygen mask first before putting the oxygen masks on her children. The needs of her patients and loved ones would have to be put on hold.

The power of visualization was illustrated with the story of the first bridge built over the Niagara River. In the beginning, one's vision of good health may be as weak as the kite string that flew across the Niagara River. Keep practicing and the image will progress to a light cord. The light cord will become a heavier cord, a rope, and finally a strong wire cable.

For a person recovering from a life threatening illness or injury, they must have a crystal clear image of their destination. "If you have good vision you can walk with confidence."

I cannot over emphasize the importance of the fitness component of any recovery program. It is my experience that the Fitness Prescription needs to be tailor-made to the needs of the individual. One size does not fit all and there is definitely no "cook book" approach. It is much more than doing exercise "A" at intensity "B" three times per week for condition "Z". The stories of Donny and Joan are a perfect example of the diversity of approaches one may utilize. Donny had to be held back and closely monitored to ensure that he was not doing too much too soon. Joan's needs were the direct opposite as she required support to get her going and to gain momentum.

In any case, the Fitness Prescription for each individual requires, at the bare minimum, that the following four questions be answered:

1. What is the individual's current health status?

2. Do they have medical clearance to perform physical exercise?

3. What is the ultimate goal for the individual's recovery?

4. Which health professional is best suited to create, supervise, coordinate and monitor the physical aspect of the recovery program? In other words, who is writing the Fitness Prescription?

IDENTIFYING A TURNING POINT

Although the recovery process is on-going, there are usually one or two elements that can be identified as keys or turning points. Joan related that it was not one key event that drastically changed her outlook on life, but rather upon how she approached each day.

Embracing the Journey of Recovery

Joan seeks her Dharma

Joan was an avid reader and especially loved the writings of Deepak Chopra. In *The Seven Spiritual Laws of Success* a whole chapter is devoted to the concept of "Dharma." Dharma is a Sanskrit word that means "purpose in life."

> *"According to this law you have a unique talent and a unique way of expressing it. There is something that you can do better than anyone else in the whole world...Each of us is here to discover our true Self to find out on our own that our true Self is spiritual...We're not human beings that have occasional spiritual experiences- it's the other way around: we're spiritual beings that have occasional human experiences."*

Joan had come a long way in her recovery but she always dreaded taking the "big test" to determine if her cancer had returned. She knew that there was a possibility that she could once again be diagnosed with cancer. Rather than living in a state of fear, Joan made a conscious choice to live each day as rich and fully as possible. The recurring questions she asked herself were:

"Who am I?"

"Why am I here?

"What is my purpose in life?"

Joan had been such a care-giver for so long that she decided to take an early retirement. It was time for her to be the care receiver and she needed time to reflect on her Dharma. On the long road of recovery, Joan made an incredible discovery. As much as she loved her nursing career, she finally realized that she was much more than her occupation and her role as a mother and a partner. She decided that she needed to look after her physical self before she could find her

Higher Self. Through all the challenges, pain and suffering, there was also joy and self discovery. By looking after herself and being grateful each day she was alive, Joan was embracing her journey of recovery.

Donny finds his "Acres of Diamonds"

Donny's story is one of looking inward and accepting the blessings of being an alcoholic.

Have you read the story called "Acres of Diamonds"?

The man who made this story famous was Dr. Russell Herman Conwell, who lived from 1843 to 1923. Conwell told this story hundreds of times and raised six million dollars in the process to help establish Temple University in Philadelphia. His dedication allowed him to fulfill his dream of building a school for poor but deserving young men.

"Acres of Diamonds" is a story about a farmer who lived in Africa at the time diamonds were discovered. One day, a visitor to his farm told him of the millions of dollars being made by men who were discovering diamond mines elsewhere on the continent. He promptly sold his farm and left on his own journey to search for diamonds.

The farmer wandered all over the African continent but never found any diamonds. He ended up penniless, in poor health and was so despondent that he threw himself into a river and drowned.

Meanwhile, the man who had bought the farmer's land came across a large rather unusual looking stone in the creek-bed which ran through his farm. He took the stone and put it on his mantel as a souvenir.

Embracing the Journey of Recovery

The same visitor, who had told the original farmer about the diamond discoveries, stopped by one day to examine the stone that the new owner had discovered. It turned out to be one of the largest diamonds ever found, and the stone was worth a king's ransom. To his surprise, the second farmer told him that his farm was covered with stones just like this one. The farm had turned out to be one of the richest diamond mines in the world. The first farmer had literally owned acres of diamonds.

> *He had made the mistake of not examining what he had in his own backyard before he ran off to look for something that he already had.*

Each of us literally has acres of diamonds around us if we will simply look for them. Like the curious appearing stones which covered the farm, they might not appear to be diamonds at first glance but with a little examination, and some polishing will reveal our opportunities for what they really are. (Reference: *Essence of Success* by Earl Nightingale)

Donny was much like the farmer in the above story. He frequently cursed his alcoholism and constantly looked for solutions and answers outside of himself. He did not see any diamonds or opportunities. In the early days of detoxification at the treatment centre he prayed that he would die. The physical symptoms, emotional turmoil and hopelessness were unbearable. At one point, he even said he'd rather have cancer. The demons of alcohol and mood altering chemicals were his master. It was a long time before he even had a flicker of hope that he could recover. The turning point for Donny came at an AA meeting when he heard a woman say that she was grateful to be an alcoholic. What kind of a stupid statement was that? He went into an absolute rampage at the absurdity of the ignorant woman. He'd rather die fighting and angry than be in a foolish and nonsensical state of bliss. How could you be happy, feel love and be connected with your fellow man when then there was so much pain and suffering?

It was in the early months of his recovery when the lights finally went on for Donny. He had always possessed a great amount of caring and empathy for others but he was now able to connect with his patients on an even deeper and more meaningful level. He was able to do this, because his pain was still very much with him. He was speaking with his heart through his hands. His gift was that he not only remembered, but had truly felt what it was like to suffer and live without hope. He was helping others heal while offering them hope. There is no greater gift in the world than to give a desperate and despondent person the inspiring message of hope. Donny finally realized that he had a precious gift to offer others.

"The ability to touch the spirit of others is the most powerful tool we have in this process of healing."

(Marg Huber-African peacemaker teacher)

Donny finally understood that his great curse was attached by an even greater blessing. Donny found "Acres of Diamonds" in his own back yard and was now grateful to be an alcoholic. If it were not for the caring and understanding of his peers, counselors and the AA program, Donny would never have discovered his incredible gift.

Embracing the Journey of Recovery

WHAT IS YOUR TURNING POINT?

Joan's turning point came through the continuing process of identifying her purpose (dharma) in life. Donny's turning point came when he discovered the acres of diamonds in his own back yard.

Have you experienced a turning point in your recovery?

Are you taking action and moving forward?

Are you learning to embrace the journey of recovery?

I truly hope you have enjoyed the experience of our journey so far.

None of us knows what the future holds for us, but let us find out where Donny and Joan are today.

Epilogue

"Do not go where the path may lead, go instead where there is no path and leave a trail."

Ralph Waldo Emerson

Epilogue

It is my hope that through the lives of Joan and Donny, you have taken to heart the words stated in the title: "Embrace the Journey of Recovery." It is very important to know where you are and where you want to go. However, it is more important to live in the moment and see, hear, touch, feel, experience and live every single moment of the journey. "Remember, it's not the destination, it's the journey."

So, where are Joan and Donny now?

There are neither fairy tale endings nor living happily ever after.

Joan and Donny met through a fortunate coincidence. Joan became a practice member of Donny's, several years after she retired from her nursing career. In the process of treating Joan for her physical condition, Donny confided in Joan that he was in a recovery program but still very afraid to tell many people for fear of the stigma attached to persons with addiction problems. Joan understood and said that for years she was afraid of telling others about wearing breast prostheses and mastectomy bras.

Embracing the Journey of Recovery

Donny was only a little over a year into his recovery process when he met Joan. The bond that developed was very healing for both of them. Joan had been through the pain and struggles of early recovery and was able to offer Donny many pearls of wisdom. And Donny's healing touch really helped Joan to the point where she would only come in for an office visit every five or six months.

It was over a year since Donny had seen Joan at the office and he wondered how she was doing. Then one day he saw Joan's obituary in the local paper. She had died of an illness unrelated to her breast cancer. He felt very sad, but the tear that rolled down his cheek was a happy tear. He knew that their meeting was no accident and that they were meant to meet and aid each other in their respective journeys.

I really miss Joan, her loyal camaraderie and her many words of wisdom.

Yes, if you haven't put it together yet, you now know that I am Donny. During this latest journey I was advised to write with the heart and edit with the mind. By combining my story with the story of Joan, the words have flowed steadily because it represents the essence of who I am. For most human beings, it is difficult to accept all of who we are. Sometimes its fun, but other times it is really scary.

I have struggled with several issues during the entire process of authoring this book. The major issue being, should I reveal to the reader that I am Donny?

Many people who suffer from chemical dependency continue to believe it is dishonorable to be addicted. They attempt to conceal, minimize or deny it. It is my experience that people suffering from mental illness and addiction fight not only the disease but the stigma attached to the disease.

Denial to admit the severity of the problem and fear of social embarrassment are two major reasons for not seeking help with alcohol and drug addiction.

The majority of the general public believes that alcoholism is caused, at least in part, by moral weakness. In fact, one of my proof-readers did not believe that **addiction was just as much an illness as cancer or heart disease.**

The American Medical Association has recognized alcoholism as a disease since 1956. Whether or not you think it is a disease or not, alcohol abuse causes over 100,000 deaths in the United States and Canada each year. (A conservative estimate to say the least)

"If we are to make real headway in treating addiction, then we must begin by recognizing that alcohol and drug dependence are not moral failings or a lack of willpower", said William C. Moyers, a recovering alcoholic and addict and vice president of External Affairs at the Hazelden Foundation for Drug and Alcohol Recovery.

"A huge way to dispel stigma is to put a face on recovery. The recovering community is invisible, largely because of this stigma", said Moyers. *It is time for people in recovery to help change the way society views addiction.*

Let them know that addiction is a disease and that treatment works

Letting others see real people with alcohol problems - people who are resourceful, articulate and creative, who are familiar already as valued friends or co-workers, people who do not fit the stereotype is a powerful way to fight stigma."

After doing some serious soul searching, I kept asking myself the following questions:

Embracing the Journey of Recovery

By revealing my story, am I operating from a consciousness of love and abundance or a consciousness of fear and scarcity?

Do I live with the stigma and keep my secret to myself or do I tell my story and let my bright light shine?

Should I focus on the shame of the past or celebrate my triumph over adversity?

I choose to play the game of life the same way as I have always played sports. I choose to play full out with my light shining brightly. If I happen to fall down, I'll ask for a hand in getting back up. But, I will always get back up so I can play full out and let my light shine once again. Then why have I been so afraid to reveal my true self? What is truly my deepest fear?

I had a deep and profound "Aha moment" recently when I read a passage about fear and being afraid.

"Our deepest fear is not that we are inadequate. Our deepest fear is that we are powerful beyond measure. It is our light, not our darkness that most frightens us... And as we let our own light shine, we unconsciously give other people permission to do the same. As we are liberated from our own fear, our presence automatically liberates others."

Marianne Williamson
"Our Deepest Fear" - A Return To Love: Reflections on the Principles of A Course in Miracles, Harper Collins, 1992. Chapter 7, Section 3

RECOVERY IS AN ONGOING PROCESS

I will leave you with one last story of my continuing journey and another important message that I have learned.

At the present time, I am thoroughly enjoying my career as a health professional. I have been together with my girlfriend for six years in a committed and caring LAT (live-alone- together) relationship. She has supported me faithfully and with rigorous honesty for my entire recovery. We would never have met had it not been for a catastrophe in her life. She tragically lost her husband at the same time I was in treatment. We have mutually supported each other in our respective recoveries and we are both grateful that the universe conspired to bring us to each other.

Every day as part of my aftercare plan, I read my mission statement which helps me stay on course. Part of the mission statement reads:

I am grateful and thank my higher power daily for the life he has given me.

I let my life be guided through my higher power and with the help of my AA recovery group.

I have made significant progress, for the most part because I have adhered to my recovery program. But, I would like to be clear that recovery is an on-going progress. There is no such mantra as, "Things are great, everything is wonderful and I don't have to bother trying anymore." During the writing of this book, I became so absorbed with my career, projects, authoring and training for the Iron Man Canada Triathlon that I forgot about working my recovery program.

For about six weeks, I chose not to have time to attend AA meetings, call my sponsor or connect with other members of the program. This is the equivalent to a diabetic not watching his diet and not taking his insulin. In other words, I did not follow my own advice and became disconnected with my recovery. Fortunately I received a slap in the face to wake me up.

It was 20 minutes into my work day when I got a message from my office manager. All it said was to call my lawyer, who had represented me in my divorce. I had no idea what he wanted to talk to me about. My calm, logical self said it did not have to be anything bad; it could have been something very trivial and harmless. However, my emotional half kept telling me something was seriously wrong.

Lawyers never call to say hello and shoot the breeze. Perhaps my ex-wife wanted something. Maybe, somebody was trying to sue me and he was giving me a warning that legal papers were coming. Maybe our office pissed somebody off and they were going to run a story about us in the local papers. I am sure that it had to be something terrible! My stomach was in knots and I felt sick and nauseated. I just had to find out what he wanted.

I tried to phone the lawyer and was told that he was busy with clients all morning. The imagined catastrophe continued to escalate. I had difficulty breathing, felt dizzy and I could barely concentrate.

The fear, anxiety and dread that I had experienced while I was using alcohol had returned. Something terrible was going to happen and there was nothing I could do about it. Every day was a struggle and near the end — it was simply a matter of surviving.

My mind immediately went to the conditioned response. The only possible solution was to hit the liquor store after work and numb these demons with a belt of Jack Daniels! Oh my God! What had happened to me? I had no intention of drinking— but my mind, body and spirit were conditioned to respond this way.

What perpetrated this supposed tragedy? It was simply the name and number of my lawyer.

Incidentally, it turned out to be a very harmless message. One of my lawyer's clients wanted to contact me and he was forwarding the request. There was no "big" catastrophe. However, there was a big lesson learned.

As I stated in the introduction and the conclusion, *"The recovery of the whole person involves the mind, body and spirit. One cannot function independently of the other. The mind, body and spirit are interconnected at all times."*

The words that I read daily were not being followed and I was disconnected from the program and my higher power. What happened to following my own mantra?

"I let my life be guided through my higher power and with the help of my AA recovery group"

In "The Big Book of Alcoholic's Anonymous", there is a quote that says, "The alcoholic at certain times has no effective mental defense against the first drink. Except in a few rare cases, neither he nor any other human being can provide such a defense. His defense must come from a higher power."

My greatest blessing is that I heeded the warning and returned quickly to working my program. I am sharing my story regularly at meetings, I am in contact with my sponsor and I have reestablished contact with my higher power.

I am trying daily to live the words I have written. With courage and humbleness I am once again embracing the journey of recovery.

Embracing the Journey of Recovery

Wherever you are on the road of recovery from a life threatening illness, I truly hope that you remember to ...

Embrace the journey...

Final Comments — About the Book Cover

The Iron Man Canada finish line photo on the book's cover reflects two crucial points on my journey of recovery. The first point of my journey began when I lay dying, despondent and disoriented in the bed of the Chemical Dependency Centre. At that point in time I was simply known as the "guy who may not make it out alive." I had just about given up all hope when something inexplicably entered my heart and soul.

A few of my peers and a counselor came to visit me that night. They said very little but their presence and their energy brought me a life changing message. I didn't hear the message, rather I felt the message.

"Go to the lights."

"Follow the energy."

Embracing the Journey of Recovery

I knew that the journey would be super difficult but I had faith confidence and belief that I was going to be okay. As long as I moved forward each day and took action I could withstand the agony of withdrawal and eventually face the world once again.

This is precisely the same feeling that I had near the finish line at Iron Man Canada. After swimming biking and running nearly 226 kilometers I was totally spent. There was nothing left in my gas tank yet I was running pretty damn fast.

My legs were aching and my stride was shortened but I was magically pulled along by the cheers from the crowd and the voice of the finish line announcer! It was dark and I had difficulty seeing where I was supposed to run. Then suddenly a familiar voice yelled out my name and gave me a high five. It was my girlfriend, Laurie! Her presence and support gave me a sudden burst of energy and it seemed as if I was sprinting to the finish line. I was so close to the finish line when the Gods played one last nasty trick on my fellow competitors and me.

We had to run past the finish line for half a mile, turn around and come back. I was so angry but even more determined not to stop. I made it to the turnaround and ran toward the finish line. The next few minutes reminded me of a near death experience. All I remember was the absolutely magnificent energy from the cheering spectators and the blinding bright lights at the finish line.

This is when I felt the same message of nearly 7 years ago.

"Go to the lights."

"Follow the Energy."

All I had to do was keep running to the bright lights and I would be home. The cheering got louder and the lights got brighter. It seemed as if everything was in slow motion as I neared the Holy Grail. Laurie snuck in front of the crowd to give me another high five as I neared the finish line. The announcer screamed out, "Here is your next winner!" I raised my arms in the air victoriously just as I had visualized a thousand times before and I felt the exquisite sensation of my torso pushing thru the finish line ribbon!

And then for one brief moment...

Life was perfect.

Free Special Offer

Note: This free special offer is available only to those people who have already purchased **"Embracing the Journey of Recovery."**

- Do you need a jump start to your recovery program?

- Do you want to develop the tenacity to move forward even in the face of seemingly insurmountable obstacles?

- Take charge of your healing journey right from the very beginning!

- Remember that you don't have to do it alone!

ACT NOW and order Dr. Larry's *Embracing the Journey* Video Series!

To receive this free, unique and innovative video coaching series ($47.00 USD value) and a 1 year subscription to the Embrace the Journey Newsletter ($27.00 USD value) follow these simple instructions:

Embracing the Journey of Recovery

1. Go to: http://Embracingthejourneybook.com

2. Click on the Bonuses icon:

3. Enter your email.

4. Enter the word "embracing" when asked for the password.

5. Press the download button and that's it. You will have immediate access to this astounding new video series.

Here are the benefits you will receive from watching this video series:

- You will discover the key ingredients to balance your mind, body and spirit

- You will develop Iron Man energy and endurance through simple daily empowering rituals

- You will discover what a successful NHL hockey player and a successful recovering alcoholic have in common

- You will determine why many alcoholics refuse to acknowledge their condition!

- You will discover the amazing secrets of health and longevity from a 4 time Stanley Cup Hockey Champion.

PS. This free special bonus offer is extremely time limited. Go to: http://Embracingthejourneybook.com and sign up now.

For More Information

- For more information on Dr. Larry's **WORKSHOPS** send an email to: info@drlarrysmith.com with **"workshops"** as the subject.

- For notification on Dr. Larry's **UPCOMING BOOKS** send an email to: info@drlarrysmith.com with **"books"** as the subject.

- For a schedule of Dr. Larry's **TELESEMINARS** send an email to: info@drlarrysmith.com with **"teleseminars"** as the subject.

- To find out how to **WORK WITH DR. LARRY ONE-ON-ONE** send an email to: info@drlarrysmith.com with **"High Performance"** as the subject.

- To book Dr. Larry **TO SPEAK TO YOUR ORGANIZA-TION** send an email to: info@drlarrysmith.com with **"Speaker Request"** as the subject.